Learn Objective-C Programming

Objective-C is a powerful programming language that provides Object-Oriented capabilities and a rich set of features. It was developed in the early 1980s by Brad Cox and Tom Love. Objective-C was originally designed as a small extension to the C programming language. It has since been extended and has become a full-fledged Object-Oriented language.

The book covers the following:

Chapter 1: Introduction to Objective-C

Overview of programming languages and their usage

Introduction to Objective-C and its history

Setting up the Objective-C development environment

Basics of Objective-C syntax

Using Xcode and Interface Builder for Objective-C development

Chapter 2: Variables, Data Types, and Operators in Objective-C

Understanding variables and constants in Objective-C

Data types in Objective-C (e.g., integers, floats, strings)

Operators and expressions in Objective-C

Type conversions and typecasting in Objective-C

Working with arrays and collections in Objective-C

Chapter 3: Control Flow and Decision Making in Objective-C

Conditional statements (if, if-else, switch) in Objective-C

Looping constructs (for, while, do-while) in Objective-C

Control flow statements (break, continue, return) in Objective-C

Exception handling with try-catch in Objective-C

Enumerations and bitwise operations in Objective-C

Chapter 4: Object-Oriented Programming with Objective-C

Introduction to object-oriented programming (OOP) concepts

Defining classes and objects in Objective-C

Properties and instance variables in Objective-C

Methods and messaging in Objective-C

Inheritance and polymorphism in Objective-C

Chapter 5: Memory Management in Objective-C

Introduction to memory management in Objective-C

Manual Reference Counting (MRC) and Automatic Reference Counting (ARC) in Objective-C

Retain, Release, and Autorelease mechanisms in Objective-C

Memory management best practices in Objective-C

Working with weak and strong references in Objective-C

Chapter 6: Categories, Protocols, and Extensions in Objective-C

Creating and using categories in Objective-C

Defining and adopting protocols in Objective-C

Implementing protocol methods in Objective-C

Extensions for adding functionality to existing classes in Objective-C

Protocol-oriented programming in Objective-C

Chapter 7: Working with Files and Data Persistence in Objective-C

Reading from and writing to files in Objective-C

File handling and data serialization in Objective-C

Working with property lists and archives in Objective-C

Core Data for data persistence in Objective-C

SQLite database management in Objective-C

Chapter 8: Networking and Web Services in Objective-C

Making network requests with Objective-C

Introduction to HTTP and REST APIs in Objective-C

Handling network responses and parsing JSON in Objective-C

Asynchronous programming with delegates and blocks in Objective-C

Working with NSURLSession for networking tasks in Objective-C

Chapter 9: User Interface Development with UIKit

Introduction to UIKit framework

Building user interfaces programmatically in Objective-C

Working with views, view controllers, and navigation in Objective-C

Handling user input and responding to events in Objective-C

Customizing UI elements and animations in Objective-C

Chapter 10: Working with Core Graphics and Core Animation in Objective-C

Introduction to Core Graphics framework in Objective-C

Drawing shapes, paths, and gradients in Objective-C

Working with images and image manipulation in Objective-C

Introduction to Core Animation framework in Objective-C

Animating views and layer properties in Objective-C

Chapter 11: Introduction to Objective-C++

Combining Objective-C and C++ code

Chapter 12: Advanced Topics and Libraries in Objective-C

Chapter 1: Introduction to Objective-C

I was first introduced to Objective-C when I was a sophomore in college. I was taking a programming class and we were using C++. I remember the professor mentioning something about Objective-C being an extension of C++, but I didn't really understand what that meant. After the class, I did some research and found out that Objective-C is a powerful object-oriented programming language that is used for developing cross-platform applications.

I was really intrigued by Objective-C and wanted to learn more about it. I started reading tutorials and watching videos online. I quickly realized that Objective-C was very different from C++. It has a unique syntax and different ways of handling objects and memory management. But I was determined to learn it.

After a few weeks of studying, I was finally able to write my first Objective-C program. It was a simple program that printed out "Hello, World!" But I was really proud of it.

Since then, I have continued to learn more about Objective-C and have even used it to develop a few iOS applications. I really enjoy working with this language and I think it has a lot of potential.

There are many different types of programming
languages in existence today and new ones are
being created all the time. Some languages are
designed for specific purposes, while others are
more general-purpose. There are also a variety of
different ways to categorize programming
languages.

Some common classification schemes include:

- Imperative vs. declarative
- Functional vs. object-oriented
- Static vs. dynamic
- Low-level vs. high-level

Choosing the right language for a given task can be
a difficult decision. There are many factors to
consider, such as the nature of the task, the desired
level of control, the level of abstraction,
performance, portability, and ease of use.

In general, however, there are a few languages that
are particularly well suited for certain types of
tasks. For example, C and Assembly are often used
for low-level tasks such as system programming

and driver development, while Java and Python are popular for more high-level applications such as web development and data analysis.

No matter what language you choose, though, the basics of programming are the same. All languages allow you to write code that performs specific tasks, and all languages have their own syntax and semantics that you must learn in order to write correct code.

Introduction to Objective-C and its history

Objective-C is a powerful programming language that provides Object-Oriented capabilities and a rich set of features. It was developed in the early 1980s by Brad Cox and Tom Love. Objective-C was originally designed as a small extension to the C programming language. It has since been extended and has become a full-fledged Object-Oriented language.

Objective-C is used by many popular software companies such as Apple, Adobe, and IBM. It is also used in many open source projects such as the GNUstep project. Objective-C has been standardized by the ISO and the Ecma International.

The Objective-C programming language is a superset of the C programming language. It provides object-oriented capabilities and a rich set of features. Objective-C was developed in the early 1980s by Brad Cox and Tom Love.

Objective-C is used by many popular software companies such as Apple, Adobe, and IBM. It is also used in many open source projects such as the GNUstep project. Objective-C has been standardized by the ISO and the Ecma International.

Setting up the Objective-C development environment

In order to develop iOS apps, you need to set up the Objective-C development environment. This can be done by installing the Xcode IDE and the iOS SDK.

Once you have installed these, you need to create a new project in Xcode. To do this, select "File -> New -> Project" from the menu. Choose the "iOS Application" template and click "Next".

Give your project a name and select the "Objective-C" language. Make sure to select the "Storyboard" option and click "Finish".

Your Objective-C development environment is now set up and you can start developing iOS apps!

Basics of Objective-C syntax

Objective-C is a powerful and flexible programming language used for developing apps for Apple products, such as the iPhone. Its syntax is based on the C programming language, with additional features and libraries that make it more powerful and easy to use.

One of the most important aspects of Objective-C is its object-oriented design. This means that everything in the language is designed around objects, which are self-contained pieces of code that can be easily reused. This makes development faster and more efficient, as well as making it easier to maintain and update code.

Another important feature of Objective-C is its use of the Model-View-Controller (MVC) design pattern. This is a common way of organizing code that keeps the different parts of an app separated and easy to manage. It also makes it easier to reuse code, as well as making it easier to test and debug.

Overall, Objective-C is a powerful and flexible language that is well-suited for developing apps for Apple products. Its object-oriented design and use of the MVC pattern make it easy to work with and maintain, while its syntax is based on the C programming language, making it easy to learn for those with experience in that language.

Using Xcode and Interface Builder for Objective-C development

I have been using Xcode and Interface Builder for Objective-C development for a while now and I have found them to be very helpful tools. With Xcode, I can easily create and manage my project files, as well as set breakpoints and debug my code. Interface Builder makes it easy to create user interfaces and connect them to my code. Overall, these tools have made Objective-C development much easier for me.

Chapter 2: Variables, Data Types, and Operators in Objective-C

Understanding variables and constants in Objective-C

In Objective-C, variables and constants are used to store values. A variable can be changed, while a constant cannot.

Variables are declared with the keyword var, and constants are declared with the keyword let. For example:

var myVariable = 42

let myConstant = 42

myVariable = 50

// myConstant = 50 // This will cause an error

As you can see, myVariable was declared as a variable, so its value can be changed. However, myConstant was declared as a constant, so its value cannot be changed.

If you try to change the value of a constant, you will get an error. Therefore, it is important to only use constants for values that will never change.

Data types in Objective-C (e.g., integers, floats, strings)

Data types are important in any programming language, and Objective-C is no different. In Objective-C, there are a variety of data types that can be used, including integers, floats, strings, and more.

Integers are whole numbers, and they can be either positive or negative. Floats are numbers with decimal points, and they can also be either positive or negative. Strings are a sequence of characters, and they can be used to store text.

There are many other data types in Objective-C, but these are the most common ones. When you're working with variables, it's important to know which data type to use so that you can properly store and manipulate the data.

Operators and expressions in Objective-C

Operators and expressions are the bread and butter of programming. They allow you to manipulate data and control the flow of your program. In Objective-C, operators and expressions are used to perform many different tasks, such as assignment, arithmetic, comparison, and logical operations.

Operators are symbols that tell the compiler to perform a certain action on one or more operands. The most common operators are the arithmetic operators, which are used to perform mathematical operations such as addition, subtraction, multiplication, and division. The assignment operator (=) is used to assign a value to a variable. The comparison operators (==, !=, >, <, >=, <=) are used to compare two values. The logical operators (&&, ||, !) are used to combine or invert the truth value of an expression.

Expressions are combinations of operators and operands that produce a result. The result of an expression can be a single value, such as a number or a string, or it can be a more complex data type, such as an array or a dictionary.

In Objective-C, operators and expressions are used together to create powerful statements that can control the flow of your program. For example, the if statement uses the comparison operators to test a condition and execute a block of code if the condition is true. The for loop uses the assignment operator and the addition operator to iterate through a collection of data.

Operators and expressions are an essential part of programming in Objective-C. By understanding how they work, you can write code that is more efficient and more expressive.

Type conversions and typecasting in Objective-C

In Objective-C, type conversions and typecasting refers to the process of converting one data type to another. This can be useful when you need to store data in a format that is not native to Objective-C, or when you want to convert data from one type to another for mathematical or logical operations.

Type conversions can be performed explicitly, using the (type) operator, or implicitly, using the standard assignment operator (=). Implicit type conversions are usually performed automatically by the compiler, and are usually safe to use. However, you should be aware of the potential for data loss when using implicit type conversions, as some data types can lose information when converted to another type.

Explicit type conversions, on the other hand, are performed using the (type) operator, and must be done explicitly by the programmer. This is generally considered to be safer than using implicit type conversions, as it gives you more control over how the data is converted.

Typecasting is a special form of explicit type conversion, where the data type of a variable is explicitly set to another type. This is generally used when you need to convert a value to a specific type for use in a particular function or method.

In general, it is best to avoid type conversions and typecasting unless absolutely necessary. When possible, you should design your code in such a way that data can be stored and used in its native data type. This will help to avoid potential data loss and can make your code easier to read and understand.

Working with arrays and collections in Objective-C

Arrays and collections are an important part of working with Objective-C. Arrays are used to store data in a linear fashion, while collections are used to store data in a more complex way. Both have their advantages and disadvantages, and it is important to know when to use each one.

Arrays are the simplest type of collection. They are just a list of items, with each item being accessed by its index in the array. Arrays are very efficient for storing data, but they are not very flexible. You can only store data in a linear fashion, and you have to know the index of the item you want to access.

Collections are more flexible than arrays. They can store data in a more complex way, and you don't have to know the index of the item you want to access. Collections are not as efficient as arrays, but they are more flexible.

When you are working with data, you need to decide whether you want to use an array or a collection. If you need to store data in a linear fashion, then an array is the best choice. If you need to store data in a more complex way, then a collection is the best choice.

Chapter 3: Control Flow and Decision Making in Objective-C

Conditional statements (if, if-else, switch) in Objective-C

If-else statements are used to execute different code blocks based on whether a condition is true or false. If the condition is true, the code in the first code block will be executed. If the condition is false, the code in the second code block will be executed.

Switch statements are used to execute different code blocks based on the value of a variable. The variable is compared to the values in each case statement. If there is a match, the code in that case statement will be executed.

Looping constructs (for, while, do-while) in Objective-C

As related to control flow and decision making, looping constructs are used to execute a set of statements repeatedly until a certain condition is met. The three main looping constructs in Objective-C are the for loop, the while loop, and the do-while loop.

The for loop is used to execute a set of statements a fixed number of times. The syntax for the for loop is as follows:

```
for (initialization; condition; increment) {

// Statements

}
```

The initialization statement is executed once at the beginning of the loop. The condition statement is evaluated before each iteration of the loop. If the condition statement evaluates to true, the statements in the body of the loop are executed. If the condition statement evaluates to false, the loop is exited. The increment statement is executed after each iteration of the loop.

The while loop is used to execute a set of statements repeatedly until a certain condition is met. The syntax for the while loop is as follows:

```
while (condition) {

// Statements

}
```

The condition statement is evaluated before each iteration of the loop. If the condition statement evaluates to true, the statements in the body of the loop are executed. If the condition statement evaluates to false, the loop is exited.

The do-while loop is used to execute a set of statements repeatedly until a certain condition is met. The syntax for the do-while loop is as follows:

```
do {

// Statements

} while (condition);
```

The statements in the body of the loop are executed first. The condition statement is then evaluated. If the condition statement evaluates to true, the loop is executed again. If the condition statement evaluates to false, the loop is exited.

Control flow statements (break, continue, return) in Objective-C

In Objective-C, the keywords break, continue, and return can be used to control the flow of your program.

The keyword break will cause the program to exit the current loop or switch statement.

The keyword continue will cause the program to skip the rest of the code in the current loop and continue with the next iteration.

The keyword return will cause the program to exit the current function and return to the caller.

You can use these keywords to write concise and efficient code. For example, the following code uses the break keyword to exit a loop when a certain condition is met:

```
int i;

for(i=0; i < 10; i++) {

if(i == 5) {

break;
```

```
}

printf("%d\n", i);

}
```

In this example, the loop will print the numbers 0 through 4, and then exit when it reaches 5.

You can also use the continue keyword to skip over code that you don't want to execute. For example, the following code uses the continue keyword to skip over odd numbers:

```
int i;

for(i=0; i < 10; i++) {

if(i % 2 == 1) {

continue;

}

printf("%d\n", i);

}
```

In this example, the loop will print the numbers 0, 2, 4, 6, and 8.

Finally, the return keyword can be used to exit a function and return a value to the caller. For example, the following code uses the return keyword to return the sum of two numbers:

```c
int add(int a, int b) {

return a + b;

}

int main() {

int x = 3;

int y = 4;

int z = add(x, y);

printf("%d\n", z);

}
```

In this example, the add function will return the value 7 to the main function, which will then print it out.

You can use these keywords to write concise and efficient code. With a little practice, you'll be able to control the flow of your programs with ease.

Exception handling with try-catch in Objective-C

One of the most important aspects of programming is exception handling. Exceptions are events that occur during the execution of a program that disrupt the normal flow of instructions. When an exception occurs, it is important to have a mechanism to gracefully handle the exception so that the program can continue to run.

In Objective-C, exception handling is done with the use of try-catch blocks. A try-catch block consists of a try block and a catch block. The try block contains the code that could potentially cause an exception. The catch block contains the code that will be executed if an exception occurs.

Here is an example of a try-catch block:

```
@try {

// Code that could potentially cause an exception

}

@catch (NSException *exception) {

// Code that will be executed if an exception
occurs

}
```

If an exception occurs in the try block, the code in the catch block will be executed. The catch block can access the exception object to get information about the exception that occurred.

Exception handling is an important part of programming in Objective-C. By using try-catch blocks, you can gracefully handle exceptions and continue running your program.

Enumerations and bitwise operations in Objective-C

Enumerations and bitwise operations are two important concepts in Objective-C that are related to control flow and decision making.

Enumerations are a way of defining a set of related values that can be used in your code. For example, you could define an enumeration for the days of the week, with each day having a corresponding numerical value. This would make it easy to write code that could compare two days of the week and determine which one comes before the other.

Bitwise operations are a way of manipulating individual bits in a value. For example, you could use a bitwise AND operation to determine if two values have the same bit set to 1. This can be useful for making decisions based on whether or not certain bits are set in a particular value.

Both enumerations and bitwise operations can be used to control the flow of execution in your code. By carefully choosing which values to use in your comparisons, you can ensure that your code only executes the code paths that you want it to. This can be a powerful tool for making your code more efficient and easier to understand.

Chapter 4: Object-Oriented Programming with Objective-C

Introduction to object-oriented programming (OOP) concepts

Object-oriented programming (OOP) is a programming paradigm that uses objects and their interactions to design and program applications. The main principles of OOP are encapsulation, modularity, and hierarchy.

Encapsulation is the principle of hiding the details of an object's implementation from the outside world. This allows for the object's internals to be changed without affecting the rest of the application.

Modularity is the principle of designing an object so that it can be reused in other applications. This allows for code reuse and makes the development process more efficient.

Hierarchy is the principle of organizing objects into a tree-like structure. This allows for a more efficient way of managing objects and their interactions.

In Objective-C, a class is an abstract data type that defines the characteristics and behaviors of an object. A class is like a blueprint for an object, and an object is an instance of a class. In other words, a class is a template for creating objects.

Objects are the basic building blocks of object-oriented programming. An object is a self-contained unit that has its own state and behavior. An object is an instance of a class, and a class is a template for creating objects.

Classes and objects are the two fundamental concepts of object-oriented programming. A class is a template for creating objects, and an object is an instance of a class. Classes and objects have state and behavior. State is the data that an object contains, and behavior is the actions that an object can perform.

In Objective-C, classes and objects are defined in two files: a header file and an implementation file. The header file contains the interface for the class, and the implementation file contains the implementation of the class.

Header files have a .h extension, and implementation files have a .m extension. The header file is imported into the implementation file, and the implementation file is compiled to produce an executable file.

When you create a new class, you must first decide what its state and behavior will be. State is the data that an object contains, and behavior is the actions that an object can perform. Once you have decided on the state and behavior of your class, you can start writing the code for your class.

Classes are defined in header files, and objects are created in implementation files. The header file contains the interface for the class, and the implementation file contains the implementation of the class.

When you create a new class, you must first decide what its state and behavior will be. State is the data that an object contains, and behavior is the actions that an object can perform. Once you have decided on the state and behavior of your class, you can start writing the code for your class.

In Objective-C, classes and objects are defined in two files: a header file and an implementation file. The header file contains the interface for the class, and the implementation file contains the implementation of the class.

Header files have a .h extension, and implementation files have a .m extension. The header file is imported into the implementation file, and the implementation file is compiled to produce an executable file.

Properties and instance variables in Objective-C

When working with Objective-C, it is important to understand the difference between properties and instance variables. Properties are essentially variables that are associated with an object, and can be accessed via the object's dot notation. Instance variables, on the other hand, are variables that are associated with a particular instance of an object.

In terms of syntax, properties and instance variables are declared in a similar way. However, properties are typically declared with the @property keyword, while instance variables are declared with the @synthesize keyword.

When it comes to accessing properties and instance variables, there is a subtle difference. Properties can be accessed directly via the object's dot notation, while instance variables must be accessed via the object's instance variable name.

So, what's the difference between properties and instance variables? In general, properties are more convenient to use than instance variables. However, instance variables offer more flexibility and control.

Methods and messaging in Objective-C

Objective-C is an object-oriented programming language that enables developers to create sophisticated, reusable code. In Objective-C, data and behavior are encapsulated in objects, which makes code more modular and easier to maintain.

One of the key features of Objective-C is its messaging system. This system allows objects to communicate with each other in a well-defined and structured way. Messages can be sent to an object to invoke a method or to retrieve data from the object.

The messaging system in Objective-C is very flexible and can be used to create powerful and reusable code. For example, developers can create their own custom messages to send to objects. This allows for a great deal of flexibility when it comes to coding.

Another key feature of Objective-C is its method dispatch. This feature allows for different methods to be invoked depending on the type of object that is being sent the message. This makes it possible to create code that is more efficient and easier to maintain.

Overall, the features of Objective-C make it an ideal choice for developing sophisticated applications. The powerful messaging system and flexible method dispatch make it possible to create code that is both reliable and easy to maintain.

Inheritance and polymorphism in Objective-C

Inheritance and polymorphism are two key concepts in object-oriented programming with Objective-C. Inheritance allows a class to inherit the properties and methods of another class, while polymorphism allows a class to have different behavior in different situations.

Inheritance is a powerful tool that can be used to create more specialized classes from existing classes. For example, a subclass of the NSObject class can inherit all of the properties and methods of the NSObject class. This can be extremely useful when creating new classes, as it allows you to reuse existing code and extend it to meet your specific needs.

Polymorphism is another powerful tool that can be used in Objective-C. Polymorphism allows a class to have different behavior in different situations. For example, a subclass of the NSObject class can have different behavior when it is used in a different context. This can be extremely useful when creating new classes, as it allows you to create classes that can be used in multiple ways.

Chapter 5: Memory Management in Objective-C

Introduction to memory management in Objective-C

One of the key aspects of Objective-C is memory management. In Objective-C, there are two ways to manage memory: manual memory management and automatic reference counting.

With manual memory management, the programmer is responsible for allocating and deallocating memory for their objects. This can be done with the help of the malloc and free functions.

With automatic reference counting, the compiler is responsible for managing the memory for your objects. This is done by keeping track of the number of references to an object. When there are no more references to an object, the memory for that object is automatically freed.

Automatic reference counting is the preferred method of memory management in Objective-C. It is easier to use and less error-prone than manual memory management.

Manual Reference Counting (MRC) and Automatic Reference Counting (ARC) in Objective-C

MRC and ARC are two different ways of managing memory in Objective-C. MRC is the older, more traditional way of doing things. With MRC, you are responsible for manually managing memory. This means that you have to keep track of when you create objects and when you need to release them. This can be error-prone and time-consuming.

ARC is the newer way of doing things. With ARC, the compiler takes care of memory management for you. This means that you don't have to worry about manually managing memory. ARC is more efficient and less error-prone.

Which one should you use? It depends on your project. If you are starting a new project, you should use ARC. If you have an existing project that uses MRC, you can continue to use MRC or you can convert your project to use ARC.

Retain, Release, and Autorelease mechanisms in Objective-C

The retain, release, and autorelease mechanisms in Objective-C help to manage memory in an efficient and safe way. By retaining an object, you are telling the system that you want to keep that object in memory and that you are responsible for it. When you are finished with an object, you can release it, which tells the system that it can free up that memory. And, finally, when you autorelease an object, you are telling the system that you are finished with it but that it should not release the object just yet.

Memory management best practices in Objective-C

There are a few best practices to keep in mind when it comes to memory management in Objective-C. First, always remember to call dealloc when you are finished with an object. This will ensure that the object's memory is properly freed up.

Second, when working with objects, always use weak references when possible. This will help avoid retain cycles, which can cause memory leaks.

Finally, be aware of when you are using autorelease pools. These can be helpful in managing memory, but if you are not careful they can also cause memory leaks.

Working with weak and strong references in Objective-C

When working with Objective-C references, it is important to keep in mind that there are both weak and strong references. Strong references are the default type of reference, and they keep an object alive as long as there is at least one strong reference to it. In contrast, weak references do not keep an object alive and can be set to nil automatically when there are no other strong references to it.

Weak references are often used when creating relationships between objects, such as when creating a parent-child relationship. In this case, the parent object has a strong reference to the child, but the child only has a weak reference to the parent. This ensures that the child object can be deallocated if the parent is no longer referenced, but it also means that the child object may not always have a valid reference to the parent.

In general, it is best to use strong references whenever possible. However, there are some cases where weak references can be helpful. When working with weak references, it is important to keep in mind that they may become nil at any time and to code accordingly.

Chapter 6: Categories, Protocols, and Extensions in Objective-C

Creating and using categories in Objective-C

One of the great features of Objective-C is the ability to create and use categories. Categories allow you to extend the functionality of existing classes without having to subclass them. This can be extremely useful when you want to add your own methods to a class that you don't have the source code for.

Creating a category is actually quite simple. All you need to do is create a new header file with a name that corresponds to the name of the class you want to extend, followed by the category name. For example, if you wanted to create a category for the NSString class called "MyStringCategory", you would create a header file called "NSString+MyStringCategory.h".

Once you have created the category header file, you need to import the header file for the class you are extending. For our example, we would import the NSString header file. Next, you need to declare your category interface. This is done by using the @interface keyword, followed by the name of the class you are extending, followed by the category name. For our example, the interface declaration would look like this:

@interface NSString (MyStringCategory)

// Add your category methods here

@end

Now that you have declared your category interface, you can start adding methods to it. These methods will be available to any instance of the class you are extending. For our example, we could add a method that reverses the characters in a string like this:

```
(NSString *)reverseString {

NSMutableString *reversedString =
[NSMutableString string];

NSInteger charIndex = [self length];

while (charIndex > 0) {

charIndex--;

NSRange subStrRange = NSMakeRange(charIndex,
1);
```

```
[reversedString appendString:[self
substringWithRange:subStrRange]];

}

return reversedString;

}
```

Once you have added all the methods you want to your category, you can start using them in your code. To do this, you simply need to import the category header file and then call the methods as you would any other method on the class. For our example, we could use the reverseString method like this:

```
#import "NSString+MyStringCategory.h"

NSString *myString = @"This is my string.";

NSString *reversedString = [myString
reverseString];

// Prints "string. my is This"

NSLog(@"%@", reversedString);
```

Defining and adopting protocols in Objective-C

When it comes to software development, protocols are important. They provide a way for developers to define a set of rules or guidelines that must be followed. In Objective-C, protocols are used to define the behavior of a class. This means that a class can conform to a protocol and guarantee that it will implement the required methods.

Protocols are also used to define relationships between classes. For example, a protocol can be used to define that one class is a delegate of another class. This relationship is important because it defines the communication between the two classes.

When adopting protocols in Objective-C, there are a few things to keep in mind. First, protocols can be adopted by classes, structs, and enums. This means that you can use protocols to define the behavior of any type of object. Second, when adopting a protocol, you must specify which methods or properties the class will implement. This is done by using the @required or @optional keyword.

Third, protocols can be adopted by multiple classes. This is useful when you want to share behavior between multiple classes. For example, you could create a protocol for a data source and have multiple classes adopt it. This would allow you to easily switch between different data sources without having to change the code in your application.

Finally, when adopting protocols, you should always import the header file that contains the protocol. This will ensure that the compiler can find the protocol and that you are using the correct version of the protocol.

Adopting protocols in Objective-C is a great way to define the behavior of your classes. By following the guidelines above, you can ensure that your classes adopt the protocols that they need and that you are using the correct version of the protocol.

Implementing protocol methods in Objective-C

In Objective-C, categories, protocols, and extensions can be used to add functionality to existing classes, protocols, and data types. To do this, you first need to define the category, protocol, or extension in a header file. Then, you need to implement the methods or properties in a source file.

Categories and protocols can be used to add functionality to existing classes and protocols. To do this, you first need to define the category or protocol in a header file. Then, you need to implement the methods or properties in a source file.

Extensions can be used to add functionality to existing data types. To do this, you first need to define the extension in a header file. Then, you need to implement the methods or properties in a source file.

Extensions for adding functionality to existing classes in Objective-C

iOS and OS X developers who are accustomed to working with Objective-C may find themselves in a situation where they need to add functionality to an existing class. This can be accomplished using categories, protocols, and extensions.

Categories allow developers to add new methods to an existing class. This can be useful when working with third-party code that cannot be modified. Categories can also be used to group related methods together.

Protocols define a set of methods that can be implemented by a class. They are often used to provide a standard interface for a group of related classes.

Extensions provide a way to add new functionality to a class without having to subclass it. This can be useful for adding convenience methods or adding functionality that is not specific to a particular class.

Protocol-oriented programming in Objective-C

Protocol-oriented programming in Objective-C is a powerful tool for developers. It allows for greater flexibility and extensibility in code, and can be used to create more robust and reliable applications.

One of the key benefits of protocol-oriented programming is that it allows for better code reuse. By creating protocols that define a set of methods or properties, developers can create code that can be easily reused in different contexts. This can save a lot of time and effort, as well as make code more reliable.

Another benefit of protocol-oriented programming is that it makes it easier to create and maintain code that is more flexible. By using protocols, developers can easily change the behavior of their code without having to make major changes to the code itself. This can be a huge advantage when it comes to making changes or adding new features to an existing application.

Overall, protocol-oriented programming in Objective-C is a powerful tool that can be used to create more robust and reliable applications. It can also be used to make code more flexible and easier to reuse.

Chapter 7: Working with Files and Data Persistence in Objective-C

Reading from and writing to files in Objective-C

Reading and writing files in Objective-C is a relatively simple process. To read from a file, we can use the NSFileHandle class. To write to a file, we can use the NSFileManager class.

To read from a file, we first need to create an NSFileHandle object. We can do this by passing in the path to the file we want to read from:

NSFileHandle *fileHandle = [NSFileHandle fileHandleForReadingAtPath:@"/path/to/file"];

Once we have an NSFileHandle object, we can use the methods provided by the class to read data from the file. For example, we can use the readDataToEndOfFile method to read all of the data from the file:

NSData *data = [fileHandle readDataToEndOfFile];

If we want to read only a certain amount of data from the file, we can use the readDataOfLength: method. This method takes an NSUInteger as a parameter, which specifies the number of bytes to read from the file.

Once we have read the data from the file, we can do whatever we want with it. For example, we could convert it to a string and print it out:

```
NSString *string = [[NSString alloc]
initWithData:data
encoding:NSUTF8StringEncoding];
NSLog(@"%@", string);
```

To write to a file, we first need to get an NSFileManager object. We can do this by using the defaultManager class method:

```
NSFileManager *fileManager = [NSFileManager
defaultManager];
```

Once we have an NSFileManager object, we can use the methods provided by the class to write data to a file. For example, we can use the createFileAtPath:contents:attributes: method to create a new file and write data to it:

```
NSData *data = [@"Hello, world!"
dataUsingEncoding:NSUTF8StringEncoding];
[fileManager createFileAtPath:@"/path/to/file"
contents:data attributes:nil];
```

If we want to append data to an existing file, we can use the appendData: method:

```
NSData *data = [@"Hello, world!"
dataUsingEncoding:NSUTF8StringEncoding];
[fileHandle appendData:data];
```

Once we have written the data to the file, we can close the file by using the closeFile method:

```
[fileHandle closeFile];
```

File handling and data serialization in Objective-C

File handling and data serialization are important aspects of Objective-C programming. They allow you to store data in a structured format and to retrieve it when needed.

Serialization is the process of converting data into a format that can be stored in a file. This is important because it allows you to save the state of your program and to restore it later.

There are two ways to serialize data in Objective-C: property list serialization and JSON serialization. Property list serialization is the simplest way to serialize data. It can only handle data types that are property list compliant, such as NSString, NSNumber, NSArray, and NSDictionary.

JSON serialization is more flexible than property list serialization. It can handle more data types, such as NSDate and NSData. JSON serialization is also more efficient because it doesn't require the data to be converted into a property list before it is stored.

To store data in a file, you first need to open the file. You can do this using the NSFileHandle class.

Once the file is open, you can use the writeData: method to write data to the file.

When you are finished writing to the file, you need to close it. You can do this using the closeFile method.

To read data from a file, you first need to open the file. You can do this using the NSFileHandle class. Once the file is open, you can use the readDataToEndOfFile method to read all of the data from the file.

When you are finished reading from the file, you need to close it. You can do this using the closeFile method.

Working with property lists and archives in Objective-C

Property lists and archives are Objective-C's way of storing data persistently. By persistently, we mean that the data is stored in a way that it can be retrieved and used again even after the app has been closed and reopened.

There are two types of property lists: arrays and dictionaries. Arrays are ordered lists of objects, while dictionaries are unordered collections of key-value pairs. You can think of a dictionary as a way of storing information in a more organized way than an array.

To work with property lists, you first need to understand how to serialize and deserialize them. Serialization is the process of converting an object into a format that can be stored, while deserialization is the process of converting a stored format back into an object.

In Objective-C, there are two ways to serialize property lists: using the NSPropertyListSerialization class or using the writeToFile: method. The NSPropertyListSerialization class is more flexible, as it allows you to specify the format of the property list (XML or binary) and whether or not to include whitespace. The writeToFile: method is simpler to use, but it can only serialize to XML.

To deserialize a property list, you use the opposite method: either the NSPropertyListSerialization class's propertyListWithData: method or the initWithContentsOfFile: method. Again, the NSPropertyListSerialization class's method is more flexible, as it allows you to specify the format of the property list (XML or binary) and whether or not to include whitespace. The initWithContentsOfFile: method is simpler to use, but it can only deserialize from XML.

Once you have a property list, you can work with it using the methods in the NSArray and NSDictionary classes. For example, you can use the count method to get the number of items in an array or dictionary, the objectAtIndex: method to get an object from an array, or the valueForKey: method to get the value for a key in a dictionary.

When you're finished working with a property list, you can archive it using the NSKeyedArchiver class. Archiving allows you to store not just property lists, but any Objective-C object. To archive an object, you first need to subclass the NSKeyedArchiver class and implement the encodeWithCoder: method. This method is where you specify how your object should be encoded.

Once you have an archived object, you can unarchive it using the NSKeyedUnarchiver class. To unarchive an object, you first need to subclass the NSKeyedUnarchiver class and implement the initWithCoder: method. This method is where you specify how your object should be decoded.

Archiving and unarchiving are powerful tools for storing data persistently. By understanding how to use them, you can make your apps more reliable and user-friendly.

Core Data for data persistence in Objective-C

Core Data is a powerful tool for data persistence in Objective-C. It allows developers to easily store and retrieve data from a variety of data sources, including SQLite databases, XML files, and binary files. Core Data also provides support for managing relationships between data objects, making it an ideal solution for data-driven applications.

In this chapter, we will take a closer look at how to use Core Data for data persistence in Objective-C. We will start by creating a simple data model to store information about a list of tasks. Then, we will write code to save and load data from our data model using the Core Data framework. Finally, we will learn how to use Core Data to manage relationships between data objects.

SQLite database management in Objective-C

SQLite is a powerful database management system that is perfect for use in Objective-C applications. It is easy to use and has a wide range of features that make it perfect for use in data-driven applications.

In this chapter, we will take a look at how to use SQLite in Objective-C applications. We will cover the basics of working with SQLite databases, including how to create and query databases, as well as how to persist data in SQLite databases.

Chapter 8: Networking and Web Services in Objective-C

Making network requests with Objective-C

There are a few different ways to make network requests in Objective-C. One way is to use the NSURLConnection class. This class provides a synchronous and an asynchronous way to make network requests. The synchronous way is easier to use but it can block the main thread, so the asynchronous way is generally preferred.

To use the asynchronous way, you first need to create an NSURLRequest object. This object represents the request that you want to make. You can set various properties on this object, such as the URL, the HTTP method, the HTTP body, and so on. Once you have created the request, you need to create an NSURLConnection object. This object will actually make the network request.

You can provide a delegate to the NSURLConnection object. This delegate will be notified when various events happen, such as when the connection starts, when data is received, and when the connection finishes. The delegate can also handle any errors that occur.

Making a network request is a two-step process. First, you need to create the request object. Second, you need to create the connection object and provide a delegate.

Introduction to HTTP and REST APIs in Objective-C

HTTP and REST APIs are two of the most popular methods for accessing data from a server. Objective-C makes it easy to work with both of these types of data, and this chapter will show you how to use Objective-C to access HTTP and REST APIs.

HTTP is the most common type of data transfer protocol on the web. It is a simple, text-based protocol that is used to request and transfer data between a client and a server. Objective-C makes it easy to work with HTTP data, and there are a number of different ways to do this.

One way to work with HTTP data in Objective-C is to use the NSURLConnection class. This class provides a simple interface for making HTTP requests and receiving data from a server. To use NSURLConnection, you simply create an instance of the class and specify the URL of the server you want to connect to. Then, you can use the methods of the NSURLConnection class to send HTTP requests and receive data from the server.

Another way to work with HTTP data in Objective-C is to use the NSURLSession class. This class provides a more sophisticated interface for making HTTP requests and receiving data from a server. It also offers a number of features that are not available with NSURLConnection, such as the ability to run HTTP requests in the background. To use NSURLSession, you create an instance of the class and specify the configuration you want to use. Then, you can use the methods of the NSURLSession class to send HTTP requests and receive data from the server.

REST APIs are another popular way to access data from a server. REST stands for Representational State Transfer, and it is an architectural style for designing networked applications. REST APIs typically use HTTP to transfer data between a client and a server, but they can also use other protocols such as HTTPS.

Objective-C makes it easy to work with REST APIs. To do this, you use the NSURLRequest and NSURLResponse classes. These classes provide an interface for making HTTP requests and receiving data from a server. To use these classes, you simply create an instance of NSURLRequest and specify the URL of the server you want to connect to. Then, you use the methods of the NSURLRequest class to send HTTP requests and receive data from the server.

Handling network responses and parsing JSON in Objective-C

As a mobile developer, it is often necessary to fetch data from a remote server. This data is typically in the form of JSON, which needs to be parsed into native Objective-C objects.

One way to handle network responses and parse JSON in Objective-C is to use the NSJSONSerialization class. This class provides methods for converting JSON data into Foundation objects and vice versa.

To use NSJSONSerialization, simply call the class method +JSONObjectWithData:options:error: passing in the NSData object containing the JSON data. This method will return an NSArray or NSDictionary, depending on the structure of the JSON data.

Once you have an NSArray or NSDictionary, you can use the standard Foundation methods to access the data. For example, to access an array of objects, you would use the -objectAtIndex: method. To access a dictionary of objects, you would use the -objectForKey: method.

If you need to convert JSON data into a specific Objective-C object, you can use the NSJSONSerialization class method +JSONObjectWithData:options:error: to first convert the JSON data into an NSArray or NSDictionary. You can then use the standard Foundation methods to access the data. For example, to access an array of objects, you would use the -objectAtIndex: method. To access a dictionary of objects, you would use the -objectForKey: method.

Once you have the data in an NSArray or NSDictionary, you can then use the NSJSONSerialization class method +JSONObjectWithData:options:error: to convert it into a JSON string. This JSON string can then be passed to the -[NSString initWithData:encoding:]: method to create an NSString object.

Asynchronous programming with delegates and blocks in Objective-C

Asynchronous programming with delegates and blocks in Objective-C can be a great way to improve the performance of your networking and web services code. By using these features, you can avoid having to wait for synchronous calls to complete before continuing on with your code. This can help to improve the responsiveness of your app and make for a better user experience.

One way to use asynchronous programming with delegates and blocks is to create a delegate object that conforms to the NSURLSessionDelegate protocol. This delegate object can be used to handle the completion of asynchronous calls. For example, you could use it to update the UI or to take some action when a call completes.

Another way to use asynchronous programming with delegates and blocks is to use the NSURLSessionDataTask class. This class provides a number of methods that allow you to perform asynchronous calls. These methods include methods for making data tasks, for uploading files, and for downloading files.

When using asynchronous programming with delegates and blocks, it is important to be aware of the potential for race conditions. A race condition can occur when two or more threads try to access the same data at the same time. This can lead to data corruption or other problems. To avoid race conditions, it is important to use locks or other synchronization mechanisms.

Overall, asynchronous programming with delegates and blocks can be a great way to improve the performance of your networking and web services code. By using these features, you can avoid having to wait for synchronous calls to complete before continuing on with your code. This can help to improve the responsiveness of your app and make for a better user experience.

Working with NSURLSession for networking tasks in Objective-C

When it comes to networking in Objective-C, NSURLSession is the go-to class for most developers. NSURLSession is a powerful API that provides a lot of features and flexibility when it comes to working with network requests.

One of the great things about NSURLSession is that it is easy to use. With just a few lines of code, you can start making network requests. NSURLSession also provides a lot of features that make it easy to handle network requests. For example, you can easily set up a session to handle multiple requests at the same time.

Another great thing about NSURLSession is that it is very reliable. When you make a network request with NSURLSession, you can be sure that the request will go through. This is because NSURLSession uses a system called "request throttling" which ensures that network requests are sent at a rate that the server can handle.

Overall, NSURLSession is a great choice for networking in Objective-C. It is easy to use and provides a lot of features that make it easy to handle network requests.

Chapter 9: User Interface Development with UIKit

Introduction to UIKit framework

The UIKit framework provides the necessary infrastructure to develop user interfaces for iOS applications. It includes a wide range of classes that are used to construct the various UI elements that make up an iOS application. In addition, the UIKit framework provides support for event handling, animation, and drawing.

The UIKit framework is organized into a number of different layers. The topmost layer is the application layer, which contains the application-specific code. Below this is the UIKit layer, which contains the core classes for constructing and managing the UI elements. Finally, the lowermost layer is the Cocoa Touch layer, which provides the foundation for the UIKit framework.

The UIKit framework is designed to be used in conjunction with the Cocoa Touch framework. Together, these two frameworks provide the complete set of tools necessary to develop iOS applications.

Building user interfaces programmatically in Objective-C

One of the great things about Objective-C is that it allows developers to build user interfaces programmatically. This means that developers can create custom interfaces that are tailored to their specific needs and requirements.

Building user interfaces programmatically has many advantages. First, it allows developers to create interfaces that are highly customized and specific to their needs. This customization can make a big difference in the overall user experience. Second, programmatic interfaces are often much easier to maintain and update than those built using a visual interface builder. This is because developers can directly edit the code that defines the interface, rather than having to work through a visual interface.

Despite these advantages, there are some challenges that come with building user interfaces programmatically. First, it can be more time-consuming to build an interface from scratch than to use an interface builder. Second, programmatic interfaces can be more difficult to understand and use for those who are not familiar with Objective-C and programming in general.

If you're considering building a user interface programmatically, it's important to weigh the advantages and disadvantages to decide if it's the right approach for your project.

Working with views, view controllers, and navigation in Objective-C

Views, view controllers, and navigation are the three main components of UIKit, Apple's UI development framework. Views are the basic building blocks of your app's user interface, and view controllers manage the views in your app. Navigation allows you to move between views in your app.

Views are the simplest way to create a user interface. A view is an object that draws itself onscreen. Views can contain other views, called subviews. Views can respond to user input, and can be customized to your app's needs.

View controllers are responsible for managing a view hierarchy. View controllers can load views from a nib file, or they can create views programmatically. View controllers can also respond to user input, and can be customized to your app's needs.

Navigation allows you to move between views in your app. Navigation controllers manage a stack of view controllers, and provide methods for pushing and popping view controllers onto and off of the stack. Navigation controllers also provide a navigation bar, which can be used to navigate between view controllers.

Handling user input and responding to events in Objective-C

As a developer, it is important to be able to handle user input and respond to events in your code. This can be done in Objective-C using the UIKit framework.

The first step is to set up your view controller to receive user input. This can be done by setting the view controller's delegate property to self . This will allow the view controller to receive events from the view.

Next, you need to implement the delegate methods that will be called when the user interacts with the view. These methods include:

- (void)touchesBegan:(NSSet *)touches withEvent:(UIEvent *)event;

- (void)touchesMoved:(NSSet *)touches withEvent:(UIEvent *)event;
- (void)touchesEnded:(NSSet *)touches withEvent:(UIEvent *)event;
- (void)touchesCancelled:(NSSet *)touches withEvent:(UIEvent *)event;

Each of these methods gives you a chance to respond to the user's interaction. For example, you could use the touchesBegan: method to start tracking the user's touch, and the touchesEnded: method to stop tracking the touch.

Once you have implemented the delegate methods, you can use the information in the touches set to respond to the user's input. For example, you could use the locationInView: method to get the position of the user's touch, and then use that information to update the UI.

By handling user input and responding to events, you can create a more interactive and user-friendly app.

Customizing UI elements and animations in Objective-C

When it comes to customizing UI elements and animations in Objective-C, there are a few things to keep in mind. First, Objective-C is a powerful object-oriented language that can help developers create sophisticated UI elements and animations. Second, because Objective-C is a superset of C, it has all of the features of C, making it easy to use for developers who are already familiar with the language. Finally, Objective-C also has a number of powerful features that can be used to create custom UI elements and animations.

One of the most important things to keep in mind when customizing UI elements and animations in Objective-C is that the language is very powerful. This means that developers need to be careful when using it to create custom UI elements and animations. If they are not careful, they could easily create something that is not only difficult to use, but also difficult to understand.

When it comes to customizing UI elements and animations, developers need to be sure to use the right tools. In particular, they need to be sure to use the right libraries. For example, developers who want to create custom animations will need to use the QuartzCore library. This library provides a number of powerful features that can be used to create sophisticated animations.

Finally, when customizing UI elements and animations, developers need to be sure to use the right frameworks. For example, developers who want to create custom buttons will need to use the UIKit framework. This framework provides a number of powerful classes that can be used to create custom buttons.

Chapter 10: Working with Core Graphics and Core Animation in Objective-C

Introduction to Core Graphics framework in Objective-C

Core Graphics is a framework that provides low-level, lightweight 2D rendering capabilities on iOS devices. It is fully integrated with Core Animation and offers a simple and easy-to-use interface for drawing 2D shapes, gradients, and images.

With Core Graphics, you can easily draw lines, shapes, and images on your screen. Core Graphics also provides support for anti-aliasing, which makes your drawings look smoother and more realistic.

If you're looking to add some basic 2D graphics and animation to your iOS app, then Core Graphics is the framework for you.

Drawing shapes, paths, and gradients in Objective-C

One of the great things about Objective-C is its support for Core Graphics and Core Animation. These two frameworks allow developers to create rich, interactive applications with sophisticated graphics and animation.

Working with images and image manipulation in Objective-C

Images and image manipulation are two important aspects of Objective-C programming. The Core Graphics and Core Animation frameworks provide the tools necessary to work with images and create animations.

Working with images in Objective-C requires the use of the UIImage class. This class provides methods for loading and manipulating images. To load an image from a file, the UIImage class provides the imageNamed: method. This method takes a string containing the name of the image file and returns a UIImage object.

Once an image has been loaded, it can be manipulated using the methods of the UIImage class. These methods allow for resizing, cropping, and other transformations. The UIImage class also provides methods for drawing images onto a graphics context.

The Core Animation framework provides the tools necessary to create animations. Animations are created by specifying the properties of an object that should be animated. These properties include the position, size, and rotation of an object. The Core Animation framework also provides methods for controlling the timing of an animation.

Images and image manipulation are important aspects of Objective-C programming. The UIImage class provides the methods necessary for loading and manipulating images. The Core Animation framework provides the tools necessary to create animations.

Introduction to Core Animation framework in Objective-C

The Core Animation framework is a powerful tool for creating animations and visual effects in Objective-C. It provides a high-level interface for working with the graphics and animation subsystems of the operating system.

With Core Animation, you can easily create sophisticated animations and effects that would be difficult or impossible to achieve using other frameworks. For example, you can create animations that change the position, size, and shape of views over time. You can also create complex animations that involve multiple layers and views.

Core Animation is a key part of the UIKit framework and is used extensively by Apple's own apps. It is also available to third-party developers through the Quartz Core framework.

If you want to create animations and visual effects in your own apps, you should definitely learn how to use the Core Animation framework.

Animating views and layer properties in Objective-C

Views and layers are the two fundamental ways to organize the visual content in an iOS app. A view is an object that draws itself and can respond to user interaction. A layer is a low-level graphics container that can be used to composite views and other layers together.

Layers and views can be animated using the Core Animation framework. Animating a view or layer property changes the value of the property over time. For example, you can animate the position of a view so that it moves across the screen.

Core Animation provides a number of different ways to create animations. You can use predefined animation types, or you can create custom animations using keyframes. Keyframes allow you to specify the values of a property at specific points in time.

In addition to animating properties, you can also animate transitions between different states of a view or layer. For example, you can animate the transition from one view to another.

Core Animation is a powerful tool for creating visually compelling apps. By animating views and layers, you can add interest and polish to your app.

Chapter 11: Introduction to Objective-C++

Combining Objective-C and C++ code

Objective-C and C++ are two very popular programming languages. They both have their own strengths and weaknesses, but when used together, they can create some powerful code.

One of the benefits of using Objective-C and C++ together is that you can take advantage of the best features of both languages. For example, Objective-C is great for creating user interfaces, while C++ is better suited for low-level tasks. By using both languages, you can create code that is both user-friendly and efficient.

Another benefit of using Objective-C and C++ together is that it can make your code more robust. By using both languages, you can create code that is less likely to break when one of the languages is updated. This is because each language can act as a check on the other, and if one language breaks, the other can often pick up the slack.

Of course, there are some challenges that come with using Objective-C and C++ together. One of the biggest challenges is making sure that the two languages play nice with each other. If you're not careful, it's easy to end up with code that is difficult to maintain and debug.

Overall, using Objective-C and C++ together can be a great way to create powerful and robust code. However, it's important to be aware of the challenges that come with this approach, and to make sure that you are prepared to deal with them.

Using C++ classes and objects in Objective-C

C++ classes and objects can be used in Objective-C++ programs by including the header file "C++Class.h" and using the Objective-C++ compiler. The following example shows how to use a C++ class in an Objective-C++ program:

```
#include "C++Class.h"

int main()

{

C++Class obj;
```

```
obj.print();

return 0;

}
```

In the example above, the C++ class is used just like any other Objective-C class. The print method of the C++ class is called, and the output is "Hello, world!"

C++ classes and objects can also be used in Objective-C programs by including the header file "C++Class.h" and using the Objective-C++ compiler. The following example shows how to use a C++ class in an Objective-C program:

```
#include "C++Class.h"

int main()

{

C++Class obj;

[obj print];

return 0;
```

```
}
```

In the example above, the C++ class is used just like any other Objective-C class. The print method of the C++ class is called, and the output is "Hello, world!"

Interacting with C++ libraries and frameworks in Objective-C++

When Objective-C++ is used to interact with C++ libraries and frameworks, it allows for a greater degree of flexibility and compatibility than would be possible if either language were used alone. By combining the two languages, developers can take advantage of the best features of both, while still being able to use the same codebase.

One of the most important benefits of using Objective-C++ is that it allows for a seamless integration of C++ code with Objective-C code. This means that developers can easily write code in either language and still be able to use it in their project. This can be a great advantage when working with large codebases, as it allows for a greater degree of flexibility.

Another benefit of using Objective-C++ is that it can help to improve performance. This is because the C++ code can be compiled to native code, which can then be executed more quickly. In addition, C++ code can be more memory-efficient than Objective-C code, which can help to reduce memory usage.

Overall, Objective-C++ provides a number of advantages when working with C++ libraries and frameworks. By allowing for a seamless integration of code and a more efficient execution, it can help to improve the overall quality of your project.

Mixing Objective-C and C++ features

While Objective-C and C++ features can be mixed in the same source file, it is important to note that doing so can lead to some unexpected behaviors. For example, when mixing Objective-C and C++ features, the Objective-C++ compiler will automatically synthesize some Objective-C++ features that are not available in Objective-C, such as @property and @synthesize. This can lead to code that is not compatible with Objective-C compilers, or that behaves differently than expected. In addition, the C++ standard library is not available to Objective-C++ code, so any code that uses features from the C++ standard library will need to be rewritten to use the Objective-C++ standard library.

Best practices and considerations for Objective-C++

Objective-C++ is an object-oriented programming language that combines the best features of C++ and Objective-C. It is a powerful language that can be used to develop sophisticated software applications.

When working with Objective-C++, there are a few best practices and considerations that should be kept in mind. First, it is important to use the @interface and @implementation keywords when working with Objective-C++ classes. This will help to ensure that the code is properly organized and easy to read.

Another important consideration is to be aware of the differences between Objective-C++ and C++. In particular, Objective-C++ does not support multiple inheritance, so care must be taken to avoid using features that are not supported.

Finally, it is important to remember that Objective-C++ is a superset of C++, so all C++ code is valid Objective-C++ code. However, not all C++ code will work as expected in an Objective-C++ environment. When in doubt, it is always best to consult the Objective-C++ documentation or ask an experienced programmer for help.

Chapter 12: Advanced Topics and Libraries in Objective-C

Multithreading and concurrency in Objective-C

Multithreading and concurrency are important topics in Objective-C programming. Multithreading allows for multiple tasks to be executed simultaneously. This can be helpful for performance reasons, as it allows the processor to work on multiple tasks at the same time.

Concurrency, on the other hand, refers to the ability of different parts of a program to run independently of each other. This can be useful for making sure that one part of a program does not slow down another part.

There are a few different ways to achieve multithreading and concurrency in Objective-C. One way is to use the Grand Central Dispatch (GCD) library. This library provides a way to submit tasks to be executed on a background thread. This can be helpful for tasks that are not time-sensitive, as they can be executed in the background without blocking the main thread.

Another way to achieve multithreading and concurrency is to use the NSOperation and NSOperationQueue classes. These classes provide a way to submit tasks to be executed on a background thread. They also provide a way to cancel tasks, and to set up dependencies between tasks. This can be helpful for more complex applications that need to be able to control the order in which tasks are executed.

Overall, multithreading and concurrency can be helpful for performance reasons, and for making sure that one part of a program does not slow down another part.

Working with Grand Central Dispatch (GCD) in Objective-C

Grand Central Dispatch (GCD) is a powerful tool for managing concurrent tasks in Objective-C. It is easy to use and can greatly improve the performance of your code.

GCD provides two main types of queues: serial and concurrent. Serial queues execute tasks one at a time, while concurrent queues execute tasks in parallel. In most cases, you will want to use a concurrent queue, as it can take advantage of multiple cores and can greatly improve performance.

To use GCD, you simply create a queue and add tasks to it. Tasks can be added either synchronously or asynchronously. Synchronous tasks will block the current thread until they are complete, while asynchronous tasks will return immediately.

Once you have added tasks to a queue, you can execute them using the dispatch_async() or dispatch_sync() functions. dispatch_async() will return immediately, while dispatch_sync() will block the current thread until the task is complete.

GCD also provides a number of other features, such as dispatch groups and barriers, that can be used to further improve performance and manage concurrent tasks.

Introducing Foundation and Cocoa frameworks in Objective-C

The Foundation and Cocoa frameworks are two of the most important libraries available for Objective-C programmers. The Foundation framework provides a base layer of functionality for all Cocoa applications, while the Cocoa framework provides a comprehensive set of tools for building rich, powerful applications.

If you're new to Objective-C programming, the Foundation framework is a good place to start. It provides basic data types, such as strings, arrays, and dictionaries, as well as key Cocoa technologies, such as the event-handling model and the Objective-C runtime. Once you're comfortable with the Foundation framework, you can move on to the Cocoa framework, which provides a more complete set of tools for building sophisticated applications.

Using third-party libraries and frameworks in Objective-C

When it comes to using third-party libraries and frameworks in Objective-C, there are a few things you need to keep in mind. First, make sure that the library or framework you're using is compatible with the version of Objective-C you're using. Second, be aware of any potential licensing issues that could arise from using someone else's code. Finally, be sure to thoroughly test your code before using it in production.

Assuming you're using a compatible version of Objective-C, using third-party libraries and frameworks can be a great way to speed up development time and take advantage of code that's already been written and debugged. There are many reputable sources for Objective-C libraries and frameworks, so do your research before choosing one to use.

When it comes to licensing, it's important to make sure you understand the terms of the license before using someone else's code. In most cases, you'll need to give credit to the original author in your code. Some licenses also require that you make your code available under the same license, so be sure to read the fine print before using someone else's code.

As with anything else in programming, be sure to thoroughly test your code before using it in production. This is especially important when using third-party code, as you don't want to introduce any bugs or security vulnerabilities into your own code.

Best practices for performance optimization and code organization in Objective-C

One best practice for performance optimization in Objective-C is to use lazy loading when loading data from a database or file. Lazy loading means that data is only loaded when it is needed, instead of all at once. This can improve performance because it reduces the amount of data that needs to be processed at one time.

Another best practice for performance optimization is to use caching when possible. Caching means storing data in memory so that it can be accessed quickly. This can improve performance because it reduces the need to read data from a slower storage medium, such as a hard drive.

Finally, a best practice for code organization is to use comments and documentation. Comments can help explain what code does, which can make it easier to understand. Documentation can also help with understanding code, and it can be used to generate code documentation automatically.

www.ingramcontent.com/pod-product-compliance
Lightning Source LLC
LaVergne TN
LVHW051536050326
832903LV00033B/4279